W9-DHX-666

brua

TEEN DISORDERS

What Is Borderline Personality Disorder?

By Alexis Burling

ReferencePoint
Press®

San Diego, CA

For more information, contact:
ReferencePoint Press, Inc.
PO Box 27779
San Diego, CA 92198
www.ReferencePointPress.com

Content Consultant: Nathaniel Herr, Associate Professor, Psychology, American University

LIBRARY OF CONGRESS CATALOGING-IN-PUBLICATION DATA

Names: Burling, Alexis, 1976- author.
Title: What is borderline personality disorder? / Alexis Burling.
Description: San Diego : ReferencePoint Press, 2021. | Series: Teen disorders | Includes
    bibliographical references and index. | Audience: Grades 10-12
Identifiers: LCCN 2020003555 (print) | LCCN 2020003556 (eBook) | ISBN 9781682829516
    (hardcover) | ISBN 9781682829523 (eBook)
Subjects: LCSH: Borderline personality disorder--Juvenile literature.
Classification: LCC RC569.5.B67 B87 2021 (print) | LCC RC569.5.B67 (eBook) | DDC
    616.85/85200835--dc23
LC record available at https://lccn.loc.gov/2020003555
LC eBook record available at https://lccn.loc.gov/2020003556

CONTENTS

Finding a Path to Healing

When writer Molly Burford of Denver, Colorado, was nineteen years old, she saw a book lying open on her parents' kitchen counter. Called *Get Me Out of Here*, it was a memoir written by Rachel Reiland about her experiences dealing with and recovering from a mental illness called borderline personality disorder (BPD). As soon as Burford saw the title, she knew she had stumbled upon something important.

"I *did* want to get out of here. Get out of my mind, get out of my life, get out of the skin I felt increasingly desperate to claw my way out of," Burford told *Glamour* magazine. "Reading the first few pages, I felt *seen*. Reiland nailed the uncontrollable sadness, the crying, the knowledge that these reactions weren't proportionate responses to whatever situation was at hand."[1]

Burford immediately searched online for "borderline personality disorder" to find out more information. The indicators

People with borderline personality disorder struggle to regulate their emotions. They may experience periods of intense sadness, especially in situations of stress.

included unstable relationships, chronic emptiness, fear of abandonment, suicidal tendencies, and others. But though she could tick off almost every symptom as

"I *did* want to get out of here. Get out of my mind, get out of my life, get out of the skin I felt increasingly desperate to claw my way out of."[1]

—*Molly Burford, a person who suffers from BPD*

Many people with borderline personality disorder also struggle with drugs and alcohol. Using substances can make it even more difficult for them to control their behavior.

something she had experienced, she decided against talking to her therapist about it. Instead, Burford kept her counseling appointments focused on her usual concerns, such as problems at school, with boys, or at home.

Over the next five years, however, Burford's condition deteriorated. Her relationships with family and friends suffered, and she had a hard time getting out of bed. She drank copious amounts of alcohol to numb the pain, and she barely ate. "I was miserable and continually suicidal; I constantly felt there was something wrong with me," she remembered. "I felt as though my life—and my mind—weren't mine. Everything felt completely and utterly out of control."[2]

Finally, when she was twenty-four, Burford hit a breaking point. Feeling like she had no other option, she told her therapist about her experience reading Reiland's memoir. She also confided that she thought she might have borderline personality disorder. After a few targeted counseling sessions, her therapist confirmed Burford's suspicions. "When the words came out of her mouth, I no longer felt resistance or fear. I just feel *understood*," Burford said. "With a diagnosis, I realized, there was a path to healing."[3]

> "When the words came out of her mouth, I no longer felt resistance or fear. I just feel *understood*. With a diagnosis, I realized, there was a path to healing."[3]
>
> —*Molly Burford, a person who suffers from BPD*

DEALING WITH BPD

According to MedlinePlus, a service of the National Library of Medicine (NLM), borderline personality disorder is defined as a mental condition in which a

Someone struggling with BPD may have an unstable view of others. He or she may experience intense periods of love and hatred toward the same person.

person has long-term patterns of unstable or turbulent emotions.

These inner experiences often result in impulsive actions and

chaotic relationships with other people. While some cases of

BPD can be minor, most tend to be debilitating, destructive, and extreme. Consequently, like Burford, many BPD sufferers often contemplate suicide.

Yet despite these unsettling circumstances, a BPD diagnosis isn't a death sentence. In fact, many people who respond to treatment can go on to live healthy, fulfilling, symptom-free lives. The first crucial step to recovery is admitting there might be a problem. Seeking professional help and gathering information about the disorder are also important. Recovering from what can be an ongoing psychological disorder can be challenging. But it is possible. "[Therapy] was hard work, emotionally grueling, but I also fully believe that it saved me. It gave me the healthy coping mechanisms I desperately needed all along," Burford said. "I still have my moments, but I can honestly say this is the happiest, healthiest, and most stable version of myself I have ever seen. The right diagnosis is a powerful thing."[4]

CHAPTER ONE

What Is BPD?

I n 1999, people across the United States flocked to their local movie theaters to see the hit film *Girl, Interrupted*. Based on a 1993 memoir by Susanna Kaysen, the movie relayed the story of a young woman played by Winona Ryder who checks herself in to a psychiatric hospital after taking fifty aspirin and drinking a bottle of vodka in a failed attempt to die by suicide. While there, she is diagnosed with BPD and spends nearly two years trying to get better.

Girl, Interrupted was nominated for a slew of awards, including a Teen Choice Award. Angelina Jolie, who played a patient diagnosed with antisocial personality disorder, won an Oscar, a Golden Globe, and a Screen Actors Guild Award for Best Supporting Actress. Teenagers loved the film's raw depiction of what it feels like to be trapped inside a psychiatric hospital with a serious mental illness.

But medical experts and critics alike condemned the movie for oversimplifying the experience of a BPD diagnosis. More than

Angelina Jolie kisses the Academy Award she won for her role in the film *Girl, Interrupted*. The popular movie was criticized by doctors for simplifying mental illnesses like BPD and antisocial personality disorder.

just a mental condition characterized by intense mood swings, wild behavior, and suicidal tendencies, borderline personality disorder is a complex illness with nuanced characteristics.

Myth vs. Fact

Since BPD was first identified in 1938, medical professionals have had a tough time defining it. Here are three common myths that persist, as well as the facts that prove them wrong, according to psychologist Paula Durlofsky.

The first myth is that people who have BPD are always difficult to be around. They are likely to be physically violent, depressed, or unable to live healthy, fulfilling lives. In fact, Durlofsky says, "These symptoms usually vary in their intensity. The majority of people diagnosed with BPD are genuinely very passionate, courageous, loyal, sensitive, thoughtful and intelligent individuals."

The second myth is that BPD is untreatable. Durlofsky explains, "The opposite is true. Current studies indicate that rates of recovery from BPD are much higher than previously thought."

The third myth is that BPD can happen at any point, and no one knows why it occurs. Durlofsky says, "BPD usually develops during adolescence or early adulthood. Trauma may be a factor in its development. Parental neglect and unstable family relationships also have been shown to contribute to an individual's risk for developing this disorder."

Paula Durlofsky, PhD, "Borderline Personality Disorder: Facts vs. Myths," Psych Central, July 8, 2018. https://psychcentral.com.

Fortunately, in the years since the disorder was officially recognized by the medical community in 1980, doctors have gained a greater understanding of what it means to live with BPD—and what it takes to get better.

BPD'S MISLEADING ORIGINS

The term "borderline personality" was first introduced in the United States by American psychoanalyst Adolph Stern in 1938. He used the phrase to describe patients who seemed to be "on the border" between neurosis and psychosis. When under stress, they exhibited certain symptoms, such as impulsivity and

near-debilitating nervousness. As stress levels declined, they were able to function normally again.

In 1980, BPD was formally listed as a psychiatric disorder in the third edition of the *Diagnostic and Statistical Manual of Mental Disorders* (*DSM-III*), a manual of mental disorders that health professionals use for diagnosis. By this time, the medical community had a more detailed grasp of what BPD entailed. Unlike what Stern and others had previously thought, BPD wasn't directly connected to neurosis, a chronic nervous condition identified by anxiety and extreme attempts to avoid panic-inducing situations. It was also unrelated to psychosis, an illness in which patients can lose touch with reality. Instead, a BPD diagnosis should be given to people who can't properly regulate their emotions specifically when dealing with other people.

For example, some people diagnosed with BPD feel intense sadness over an interaction and can't move on from that feeling. Others experience ongoing emptiness or sudden periods of intense, irrational anger. "Unlike other psychiatric diagnoses, if you put someone with schizophrenia on an island all by themselves, their mental illness would still be evident," explained Dr. Perry D. Hoffman, president and cofounder of the National Education Alliance for Borderline Personality Disorder (NEABPD). "If you put someone with BPD on an island, you wouldn't necessarily see the symptoms—whatever happens, happens in the context of [interacting] with someone else."[5]

Today experts are still learning about BPD, its causes and symptoms, and how it affects different people before, during, and after treatment. They've also discovered that it's not as uncommon as they once thought. In fact, according to the NEABPD, an estimated 5.9 percent of adults in the United States have experienced BPD at some time in their

life. BPD affects 50 percent more people in the United States than Alzheimer's disease, and nearly as many as schizophrenia and bipolar disorder combined. Twenty percent of patients admitted to psychiatric hospitals and 10 percent of people in outpatient mental health treatment are diagnosed with BPD.

GENDER DIFFERENCES

According to the NEABPD, approximately 14 million adults in the United States have been diagnosed with BPD at one point in their lifetime. The National Alliance on Mental Illness (NAMI) further states that nearly 75 percent of these people are women.

But other studies suggest these figures might be inaccurate or at least misleading. For one, it is possible that women are simply more likely to seek treatment, explaining why they are diagnosed more often. "While BPD is reported to be more prevalent in women than men, that is not correct," says John

BPD is more commonly diagnosed in women than in men. However, this may be due to societal biases that cause psychiatrists to view women as being more emotional than men.

Oldham, MD, professor of psychology at Baylor College of Medicine in Houston. "What is correct is that patients in clinical treatment settings are much more likely to be women than men."[6]

Because women tend to be more comfortable than men expressing their feelings openly, clinicians might be more likely to diagnose women with BPD. "There's definitely a bias in the field. Some of it has to do with how we are socialized in our

"While BPD is reported to be more prevalent in women than men, that is not correct. What is correct is that patients in clinical treatment settings are much more likely to be women than men."[6]

*—Psychology professor
John Oldham, MD*

culture at large. Clinicians can also fall into this bias," says Jill Weber, a psychologist in Washington, DC.[7] What that means is while BPD might be more common in women in clinical environments, there may actually be an equal number of men and women with the disorder out in the world.

DUAL DIAGNOSES

In addition to discrepancies regarding gender, it can also be difficult to definitively diagnose BPD because the illness often coexists alongside other psychological conditions. According to the National Institute of Mental Health (NIMH)–funded National Comorbidity Survey Replication, which is the largest national study to date of mental disorders in US adults, about 85 percent of people with BPD also suffer from a different mental illness. For example, 70 percent of adults with BPD also struggle with dysthymia, a chronic type of depression. Sixty percent have

BPD VS. BIPOLAR DISORDER

Getting the right diagnosis isn't easy for psychiatric conditions, especially if two illnesses exhibit similar symptoms. Here is a quick explanation of the differences between two often misdiagnosed disorders:

Borderline Personality Disorder	Bipolar Disorder
• A long-standing pattern of abrupt, moment-to-moment mood swings • Mostly affects the regulation of emotions, not specifically sleep or energy levels • Stormy personal relationships, extreme fear of rejection, unstable self-image, emotional instability, impulsivity leading to reckless behavior, and self-harm or suicidal behavior • Mood swings triggered by conflicts in interactions with other people	• Alternating periods of depression and mania that can last from days to months • Manic episodes characterized by diminished need for sleep, excessive talking, racing thoughts, delusions of grandeur, intense pursuit of pleasurable activities often with painful consequences • Depressed episodes characterized by prolonged sad mood, loss of interest in pleasurable activities, significant weight loss or gain, too much or too little sleep, either lethargic or agitated movements, decreased concentration, preoccupation with suicide • Mood swings not triggered by interpersonal conflicts

major depressive disorder, 25 percent have antisocial personality disorder, and 15 percent are diagnosed with bipolar disorder.

Beyond specific psychiatric illnesses, people with BPD often exhibit self-destructive behavior. Thirty-five percent are addicted to drugs or alcohol. Twenty-five percent have unhealthy relationships with food and have bulimia, anorexia, or problems with binge-eating. Approximately 55 to 85 percent percent practice cutting or other types of self-harm. Because these symptoms, behaviors, and other mental conditions often overlap, properly diagnosing and treating BPD becomes that much harder.

BPD IN TEENS

Possibly the most controversial topic when considering BPD is whether it can be diagnosed in someone younger than eighteen. Adolescence is a period of major developmental transitions—physically, psychologically, and socially. Teens are naturally prone to mood swings, risk-taking behavior, and bouts of anxiety, insecurity, or nervousness due to the onset of puberty. For parents, educators, and doctors, it can be difficult to differentiate between a run-of-the-mill episode of teenage angst and a true BPD diagnosis. For this reason, up until recently, most clinicians were wary about diagnosing BPD in adolescents.

Symptoms of BPD and self-harm can begin in young teenagers. Some people exhibit behaviors of BPD by the age of twelve.

But some medical professionals have started to change their opinions on the subject. For them, there's a big difference between minor tantrums or periodic overreacting and a clear pattern of self-destructive behavior. "Many teenagers have a day or even a few days when they get upset and slam a door or curse at their parents," explains Dr. Alec Miller, professor of clinical psychiatry and behavioral sciences and chief of child and adolescent psychology at Montefiore Medical Center at the Albert Einstein College of Medicine. "But teens with borderline personality disorder engage in more extreme behavior—and more often—than the average teen, and these behaviors impair their social, school and working lives."[8]

> "Many teenagers have a day or even a few days when they get upset and slam a door or curse at their parents. But teens with borderline personality disorder engage in more extreme behavior—and more often—than the average teen, and these behaviors impair their social, school and working lives."[8]
>
> —Clinical psychiatry and behavioral sciences professor Dr. Alec Miller

For example, while it's common for adolescents to bicker with their siblings, a fifteen-year-old boy with BPD might get in a fight with his older brother, feel intensely angry, then lock himself in his room to self-mutilate or overdose on the pills stashed in his night table drawer. A sixteen-year-old girl with BPD might feel depressed or lonely and drink seven beers in an hour or engage in promiscuous sex, which could result in pregnancy. "The point here is that these teens' extreme behavior typically follows their inability to tolerate negative emotions like anger," Dr. Miller says.[9]

For Dr. Miller and others, diagnosing BPD sooner rather than later has become increasingly important. They feel that waiting too long to address the issue can negatively impact development. "Take a person with extremely strong, intense emotions, who is constantly told that she's overreacting, she shouldn't feel the ways she feels," says Dr. Jill Emanuele, clinical psychologist and director of the Mood Disorders Center at the Child Mind Institute. "As a result, she doesn't learn how to regulate and modulate her emotions."[10]

Another reason to either diagnose or rule out BPD early is that it will help determine whether other mental conditions are present, such as attention-deficit/hyperactivity disorder (ADHD), depression, or bipolar disorder. It will also prevent teenagers from being inappropriately prescribed a range of medications that can have significant side effects. "I've seen kids with BPD who were on extensive drug cocktails because the clinicians didn't know what was happening," warns Dr. Emanuele. "They're just going after the symptoms. And no medication is going to correct the invalidation that these people feel."[11]

"I've seen kids with BPD who were on extensive drug cocktails because the clinicians didn't know what was happening. They're just going after the symptoms. And no medication is going to correct the invalidation that these people feel."[11]

—Clinical psychologist Dr. Jill Emanuele

Dealing with a BPD diagnosis can be time-consuming and difficult. Like any mental illness, it comes with a stigma. But there is hope for teens and adults who struggle with the condition. Working with a medical professional to learn why it happens, how to spot the symptoms, and where to go for treatment is the key to forging a healthy, productive future.

CHAPTER TWO

What Are the Symptoms and Causes of BPD?

In February 2010, an unnamed woman wrote a letter to the *New York Times* in response to an article about BPD. In the note, she explained she was having trouble with her temperamental fifteen-year-old son and didn't know where else to turn. When he was ten years old, he had been diagnosed with generalized anxiety disorder and ADHD. He was assigned a psychiatrist and was put on a slew of antipsychotic and antidepressant medications, including Concerta, Abilify, Lamictal, and Celexa.

After going to a few therapy sessions and adjusting to the drugs' effects, her son's condition had improved. But when he turned thirteen, circumstances changed. His grades dropped.

Someone with BPD may act impulsively. He or she may react with extreme amounts of anger to small criticisms or inconveniences.

He started hanging out with rowdy kids from out of town. His mother and father suspected him of abusing drugs and alcohol. His behavior continued to get worse. Now, two years later, she felt more confused than ever about what to do next.

Mental health professionals are able to provide a diagnosis to those suffering from mental illnesses. It is important to visit a psychiatrist or other professional if people become a danger to themselves or others.

"We have tried to be 'loving and understanding' parents, but his outbursts, manic behavior with his bouts of depression, and his sense of emptiness are taking a toll on our family," she wrote. "I wonder if we are on the right path: does he have borderline personality disorder?"[12] She signed the letter "Overwhelmed mother."

As demonstrated in this situation, properly identifying a mental illness can be confusing, especially when it involves emotions and mood regulation. Like some other psychiatric illnesses having to do with the brain, there unfortunately isn't a specific laboratory, blood, or genetic test a patient can take to find out definitively whether he or she has BPD. A BPD diagnosis isn't based on one defining sign or characteristic either.

But making an appointment with a licensed mental health professional is a good way to get some answers. Most people who have BPD are diagnosed with the condition after a formal assessment. During these sessions, the psychiatrist or therapist looks for common characteristics that point to a BPD diagnosis. Though a clearly evident diagnosis can take a while to pin down, there are a few major symptoms to be aware of with BPD.

MENTAL AND EMOTIONAL SYMPTOMS

According to the *DSM*, there are nine key symptoms to look for when determining whether one of the four borderline personality disorder types is present. In order for a person to receive a positive diagnosis, he or she needs to exhibit at least five out of the total nine. One is a tendency to worry about being rejected by family and friends, taking extreme measures to prevent that scenario from playing out. "[People with BPD] experience intense abandonment fears, even when faced with a realistic time-limited separation or when there are unavoidable changes in plans," says John M. Grohol, a journalist for Psych Central. "For instance, a person with this condition may experience sudden despair in reaction to a clinician's announcing the end of the hour; or panic and fury when someone important to them is just a few minutes late or must cancel an appointment. They may believe that this 'abandonment' implies that they are a 'bad person.'"[13]

> "[People with BPD] experience intense abandonment fears, even when faced with a realistic time-limited separation or when there are unavoidable changes in plans."[13]
>
> —*John M. Grohol, a journalist for* Psych Central

Another major symptom, sometimes called "splitting," is a pattern of unstable personal relationships that alternates between idolization and what's called devaluation. For example, one day a person with BPD is obsessed with a romantic partner and wants to be as close to the partner as possible at all times. The next day, the person with BPD thinks

Splitting causes someone with BPD to have two extreme and opposite views of another individual. The person is unable to reconcile these conflicting viewpoints, which can cause difficulties in relationships.

his or her partner is worthless and is ready to break up over something inconsequential.

This flipping back and forth between thoughts is hard on everyone involved. "Historically, people with BPD have been viewed as purposely manipulative, using extreme measures to get things, gaming people around them," says Dr. Emanuele. "But that's not it at all. These people are in intense pain, and feel they can't get what they need."[14]

Another symptom to watch out for is a sudden change in self-identification. This can affect a person's moods, opinions, goals, and relationships with other people. For example, a young boy with BPD might start out the week believing he is the smartest student in his grade and that he deserves to be class president. An offhand comment from a teacher about being late for algebra, however, might cause him to lose confidence and rethink his self-image. By the middle of the week, he's skipping class because he now believes he's the class loser.

Above all, BPD is defined as a roller-coaster ride of strong emotions. A person with the condition can go through phases of intense depression, severe anxiety, or irritability. She might experience chronic feelings of boredom, apathy, uselessness, and emptiness. Paranoid thoughts, especially during high-stress periods, are also common. Unlike bipolar disorder, in which a manic or depressive episode can go on for a few weeks, the strong emotions experienced by people with BPD usually last anywhere from a few minutes to a few hours but rarely for more than a few days.

BEHAVIORAL SYMPTOMS

On top of the emotional upheaval, many people who suffer from borderline personality disorder struggle with behavioral changes. Some are prone to violent outbursts fueled by inappropriate anger or uncontrollable rage, followed by shame or guilt. "The reason anger in BPD is called 'inappropriate,' is because the level of anger seems to be more intense than is warranted by the situation or event that triggered it," says Dr. Kristalyn Salters-Pedneault, a clinical psychologist and associate professor of psychology at Eastern Connecticut State University. "For example, a person with BPD may react to an event that may seem small or unimportant to someone else, such as a misunderstanding, with very strong and unhealthy expressions of anger, such as yelling, being sarcastic, or becoming physically violent."[15]

> "A person with BPD may react to an event that may seem small or unimportant to someone else, such as a misunderstanding, with very strong and unhealthy expressions of anger, such as yelling, being sarcastic, or becoming physically violent."[15]
>
> —Dr. Kristalyn Salters-Pedneault, a clinical psychologist and associate professor of psychology at Eastern Connecticut State University

People with BPD tend to be impulsive. This impulsivity can lead them to reckless behavior, such as gambling or drug use.

Two of the most damaging symptoms of BPD include a tendency for recklessness or impulsivity and a propensity for self-harm. People suffering from BPD often abuse drugs or alcohol, drive irresponsibly, have unsafe sex with strangers, gamble, or sabotage their own success in relationships or jobs.

In an effort to reduce or control intense emotions, many people with BPD engage in self-harm or disordered eating habits such as bingeing and purging or restricting food intake. "In personality disorders, this enduring pattern of behavior is inflexible and pervasive across a broad range of personal and social situations. It typically leads to significant distress or impairment in social, work or other areas of functioning," notes Grohol.[16]

Perhaps the most dangerous symptom of BPD is a susceptibility to suicidal thoughts. Research shows that as many as 80 percent of people with BPD will

The Risk of Suicide

When Cassandra Hill turned twenty-six in 2019, she was surprised she was still alive. For as long as she could remember, she had suffered from severe anxiety and depression. She told herself she was "broken" and "worthless." Soon, she started cutting herself to "regulate the pain."

The suicidal thoughts began after Hill entered high school. Though her therapist prescribed medication, the pills soon stopped working. She tried to kill herself twice in two years.

After a third attempt to kill herself, Hill was placed in an outpatient program and was diagnosed with BPD. "I finally found out there was an actual reason for all my extreme behaviors. It explained why 'abandonment' diminished my self-worth, why I want to hurt myself, why I'm impulsive and why my relationship patterns are so tumultuous," she said. "It explained everything. It explained how trauma had shaped my life."

Suicidal thoughts are life threatening. But there are professionals who can help. The toll-free National Suicide Prevention Lifeline (NSPL) can be reached at 1-800-273-TALK (8255), twenty-four hours a day, seven days a week. The service is available to everyone. People who are deaf or hard of hearing can contact the Lifeline via TTY at 1-800-799-4889. All calls are free and confidential.

Cassandra Hall, "I'm Still Here," National Alliance on Mental Illness, *September 4, 2019. www.nami.org.*

make at least one suicide attempt in their lifetime, and most of those people will make more than one. People with BPD are also more likely to die from suicide than individuals with any other psychiatric disorder. Between 8 and 10 percent of people with BPD die by suicide, which is more than fifty times the rate of suicide in the general population.

"BPD is associated with very intense negative emotional experiences. These experiences are so painful that many people with BPD report that they would like to find a way to escape. They may use a number of different strategies to try to reduce their emotional pain, such as deliberate self-harm or substance use and even suicide," says Dr. Salters-Pedneault.[17]

CAUSES

Doctors don't know exactly why BPD occurs in some people and not in others. But most agree that it has to do with a combination of factors. There are three key influences that can contribute to a positive diagnosis. The first is genetics. According to NAMI, though no specific gene profile points directly to BPD, people who have a close family member with the disorder—a parent or sibling—may be at a higher risk of developing it.

Environmental and social factors can be contributors, too. Many people with BPD report going through traumatic life events, such as sexual or physical abuse, neglect, bullying, or

Home life and family relationships can influence the development of BPD. For example, it can be difficult to have a stable relationship with a parent who struggles with substance addiction.

other types of adversity, during childhood. Some may have been exposed to unstable and toxic relationships, such as a parent with a violent temper or a caregiver with an addiction problem.

BPD and the Brain

In May 2019, the results of a small but groundbreaking study were released to the public. According to Harold W. Koenigsberg, MD, professor of psychiatry at Mount Sinai School of Medicine, people with BPD might be physically unable to regulate emotion.

In the study, researchers used brain-imaging scans to investigate how the brains of people with BPD reacted to social and emotional stimuli. First, they showed a group of people with BPD images of a disturbing emotional scene. Then they watched what happened on the brain-imaging screens. When the subjects attempted to control or lessen their reactions to what they saw, areas of the brain that are normally active in healthy people under the same conditions remained inactive in the BPD patients.

"This research shows that BPD patients are not able to use those parts of the brain that healthy people use to help regulate their emotions. This [also] may explain why their emotional reactions are so extreme," said Dr. Koenigsberg. "Studying which areas of the brain function differently in patients with borderline personality disorder can lead to more targeted uses of psychotherapy and medications, and also provide a link to connect the genetic basis of the disorder."

Rick Nauert, PhD, "Brain Scans Clarify Borderline Personality Disorder," Psych Central, May 3, 2019. www.psychcentral.com.

The third potential cause of BPD is a difference in brain function when compared to people without any mental or personality disorder. Studies show that the brains of people with BPD can be structurally different, especially in the areas that control impulses, decision-making, and emotional regulation. Another possibility is that the brain has low levels of serotonin or doesn't process mood-regulating chemicals properly. Serotonin is a chemical in the brain that regulates emotion, temperature, and appetite. It can also suppress aggressive or antisocial behaviors.

Scientists are still researching what causes BPD and how it might be prevented. As with all mental conditions, though these risk factors might be present, they are not definite precursors to BPD. There are also many people without a genetic predisposition to the disease or a childhood trauma who will develop BPD at some point in their lifetime. The disorder affects all aspects of daily life, including social interactions, family relationships, productivity and job preparedness, and the ability to form and follow through on goals.

CHAPTER THREE

How Does BPD Affect Daily Life?

When Erika Lee entered college in 2014, her experience seemed much like any other young person's. She obsessed over her love life, which parties to attend, and how to improve her grades. At night, she talked to her boyfriend for hours about everything from her classes and new friends to her dreams for life after school.

But even though everything looked normal on the surface, the way Erika felt inside was always in turmoil. "My relationships constantly fluctuated—getting people to want to date me or be my friend was easy, but people never seemed to want to stick around," she wrote in an article for HuffPost about her experience with BPD. "No matter how great my life was, or how many people cared about me, I always felt empty and unloved. When my friends weren't with me, I was always paranoid they would be saying things behind my back. I had no logical reason

People with BPD may worry excessively if their friends do not text back immediately. They may believe their friends hate them or have abandoned them.

for these feelings, but I always felt like everyone was against me."[18]

Though Erika didn't realize it at the time, telltale patterns

"No matter how great my life was, or how many people cared about me, I always felt empty and unloved."[18]

—Erika Lee, a person who suffers from BPD

Parenting with BPD

In Erika's situation, her mother was the person who suggested she see a psychiatrist for help. But what happens when a parent or guardian is the one with BPD? How does the diagnosis affect parenting and the quality of life in the home?

Licensed clinical psychologist Natalie Feinblatt suggests that if a parent or guardian has BPD, the home environment is often ruled by anxiety. Anger flare-ups are common. Relationships become strained. In some cases, it can be difficult to figure out which of the parent's emotions are playing out at any given moment, which can be confusing for kids. "[Your mother] either loves or hates you with a passion. And when she feels one way about you, she will fail to remember or even deny that she ever felt any other way," Feinblatt says.

Health and wellness expert Caleb Backe describes another pervasive problem: a switch-up in power dynamics that has a long-term effect on development. Essentially, the parent becomes the kid. "Sometimes, there will be a role reversal situation, where the daughter is sought by the mother for strength and comfort, rather than the other way around," he says. "Coupled with the BPD tendency to suffer from abandonment issues, it can get very tense and very unstable—fast."

Carolyn Steber, "11 Subtle Signs Your Mom Might Have Borderline Personality Disorder," Bustle, *November 22, 2017. www.bustle.com.*

had developed in her behavior. Whenever a friend or boyfriend didn't text her back, she panicked. She assumed they were ignoring her on purpose or hanging out with someone better. When she confronted them, an argument or emotional meltdown almost always followed. Some of her relationships never recovered.

Then, during her junior year, something life-changing happened. She had just gotten into a fight with her parents about skipping too many classes. But instead of punishing her, Erika's mother suggested they sit down to talk. "She had noticed that I had been crying almost every morning

People with BPD are often criticized for being dramatic or seeking attention. However, recognizing their emotions and offering support can help lead to improvements in behavior.

for almost no reason and had no motivation to get out of bed. She was worried that I would fail all my classes," Erika recalled. "At first, it felt like she only cared about how I was doing in school and not actually how my health was. But after saying I was fine for a few months and not actually being fine, I realized it didn't matter because I couldn't go on like this."[19]

After the heart-to-heart with her mother, Erika agreed to see a psychiatrist and was soon diagnosed with BPD. She went on medication and began psychotherapy, which helped. Though her issues didn't resolve themselves overnight, she noticed a small, gradual improvement in how she felt inside. She stopped waking up in tears. Her days seemed to be more fulfilling and emotionally balanced. Though not all of her friends forgave her for acting erratically and some of them felt she was too difficult to be around even with an official diagnosis, her relationships got better little by little.

By 2019, after two years of treatment and learning healthier coping mechanisms, Erika's circumstances had changed considerably. Instead of lashing out at others, she approached situations calmly and with a level head. When facing an emotional roadblock, she asked for help instead of assuming the worst of those around her. Most importantly, her outlook on her future was more positive than it had been in years.

"The truth is that I, along with others who struggle with BPD, just want to feel seen and heard and be believed in," she wrote. "I'm doing my best to make sure that I am becoming a better version of myself every single day. My greatest wish is to attain stability—emotionally, physically and mentally. BPD isn't untreatable; it just takes time."[20]

UNSTABLE RELATIONSHIPS

As Erika found out the hard way, BPD can take a devastating toll on relationships if left untreated. Because people with the condition have trouble regulating and processing their emotions, navigating interactions with other people often seems like a minefield fraught with tension and potential for failure. In many cases, friendships, romantic partnerships, and familial relationships suffer from ongoing friction and periods of undue stress. In extreme situations where physical or mental abuse occurs, the breakup of a friendship or relationship is often the end result.

On the flip side, some BPD sufferers try to convince themselves that everything in their life is perfect to counteract their flip-flopping personality. When it doesn't turn out that way, they erupt in anger and often blame others for their shortcomings. "Their emotions are like exposed nerve endings. Those with BPD have a distinctively polarized view of relationships, idealizing themselves and others, but one mistake,

"I'm doing my best to make sure that I am becoming a better version of myself every single day. My greatest wish is to attain stability—emotionally, physically and mentally. BPD isn't untreatable; it just takes time."[20]

—Erika Lee, a person who suffers from BPD

Patterns of Destruction

Six months after her mother's suicide, Sarah Haufrect was still thinking about what she could have done to prevent it. But Haufrect had tried her best. Though it took a while for her to believe it, she now understood that nothing would've been enough.

Haufrect's mother had lived for more than sixty years with a mental illness. Though she was never officially diagnosed, the signs for BPD were all there. She tried to stab her first husband—Haufrect's father—with a kitchen knife. He divorced her. After fifteen years of another tumultuous marriage, her second husband left, too. She developed alcoholism and went bankrupt. Most of her friends refused to return her calls. Her second daughter stopped speaking to her altogether.

A week before Haufrect's mother died, she gave Haufrect a grill. When Haufrect tried to put it together, her mother berated her for doing it incorrectly. "When I look back on that day, this is what I see: the years of trying eventually gave way to the years of accepting that she was never going to get better," Haufrect recalls. "She was not only unwilling, but also unable."

Sarah Haufrect, "I Loved, Lived With, and Lost My Mother to Borderline Personality Disorder," Salon, February 29, 2016. www.salon.com.

and the person is totally devalued," explains Dr. Helen Grusd, past president of the LA County Psychological Association and a forensic and clinical psychologist for more than thirty years. Living with a person with BPD is, in Dr. Grusd's words, "like living with Mount Vesuvius always on the verge of erupting."[21]

Younger people especially have a difficult time coping with BPD, particularly if the situation is unstable at home. "Some children need more than others in learning to regulate their emotions," says Marsha M. Linehan, a psychologist at the University of Washington. "They do best with stability. If the family situation is chaotic or the

BPD can increase tensions within a household. It can be especially challenging for children to deal with this added stress.

family is very uptight, teaching children to grin and bear it, that tough kids don't cry, these children will have a lot of trouble."[22]

PRODUCTIVITY PROBLEMS

In addition to disrupting relationships with other people, a BPD diagnosis can also impact a person's internal development.

Someone with BPD may change jobs often. Splitting can affect relationships with coworkers or cause people to lose their jobs.

Some people with BPD experience difficulty staying focused when completing a task or assessing what needs to be done to correctly solve a personal problem or work situation. While a holdup or disagreement at the office might be a temporary annoyance for someone without BPD, for someone with BPD, it could be a serious setback. In these situations, a small misunderstanding could easily trigger the person to erupt in anger, to lash out, to blame everyone else, or to turn all of that criticism onto themselves.

What's more, many people with BPD have trouble holding down a job, attending school consistently and earning a degree, or even doing something as minor as sticking with a hobby to see it through to fruition. This affects not only their short-term self-confidence but also their ability to set long-term goals and envision a fulfilling life in the future. Licensed clinical social worker Erin Johnston uses the story of a man named Bruce as a case study example. Bruce has BPD and a history of job changes that play out in a discernible pattern. First, he gets hired and is obsessed with the job. Then he starts to see every work request as "unfair criticism" while also feeling like his coworkers are lazy. Soon, he's convinced everyone is picking on him and "out to get him." Then he flies into a rage, telling his boss he has "always" been discriminated against. The disrespectful outburst causes him to get fired.

"Bruce's initial feelings towards his coworkers and boss are intense and idealized. He sees them as doing no wrong and as strong allies who like and support him. However, these feelings soon give way to negative, critical thoughts. Now Bruce sees nothing positive about the people he works with, instead, experiencing them as hostile backstabbers," Johnston says. "Splitting is a defense mechanism common in people with BPD. Instead of seeing another person as primarily good with a few bad traits, the shift to 'bad person' is complete in an effort to avoid the possibility of rejection."[23]

RISKY BEHAVIOR

Perhaps the most dangerous long-term impact of living with BPD is its potential for inciting self-damaging or life-threatening behavior. As a result of their raging emotions, suicidal thoughts, fear of abandonment, or impulsivity, people with BPD might have multiple altercations with the police or face jail time. In fact, according to Dr. Salters-Pedneault, about a third of people with BPD will be convicted of a crime in their lifetime.

One cause of legal trouble is impulse control. "If you have BPD, you may struggle with taking actions without thinking about the consequences or engaging in behaviors when you

BPD may make it more likely for people to engage in illegal impulsive behaviors, such as shoplifting. These behaviors can have severe legal consequences.

are angry or upset," Dr. Salters-Pedneault says.[24] Shoplifting, reckless driving, and prostitution are all examples of impulsive behaviors that are also illegal.

Many who struggle with BPD also struggle with addiction. Around two-thirds of those diagnosed with BPD have also attempted to use drugs as a form of self-medication.

Another source of run-ins with the law is any form of physical violence, including domestic abuse, child abuse, and neglect. Relationships with high levels of conflict are a central feature of BPD. This can result in a messy divorce, custody battles, and even a restraining order if a partner or parent becomes aggressive. "Very intense emotions, including borderline rage, can drive someone with BPD to abuse his children or to be so consumed with his own emotions that he neglects his children's care," Dr. Salters-Pedneault says. "Some are so impaired by their symptoms that they engage in criminal abuse and neglect, sometimes leading to arrest and incarceration."[25]

Finally, while a substance abuse problem might not always result in an arrest, it can cause serious damage to not only the person suffering from BPD who is doing the drug but also the people around him or her. Alcoholism or drug abuse is unhealthy for the body, and when coupled with risky behavior such as reckless driving or unprotected sex, it can cause irreparable harm.

> "Very intense emotions, including borderline rage, can drive someone with BPD to abuse his children or to be so consumed with his own emotions that he neglects his children's care."[25]
>
> —Dr. Kristalyn Salters-Pedneault, a clinical psychologist and associate professor of psychology at Eastern Connecticut State University

Duke University psychology student Bisma Suleman knows the problems impulsivity can cause all too well, having suffered with BPD for most of her life. "People with BPD are known to be

BPD can cause feelings of profound emptiness and hopelessness. However, treatments for this disorder are available.

very impulsive," she wrote in a blog post for NAMI. "However, the root cause of this is important, too. One of the many symptoms of BPD is chronic feelings of emptiness. This isn't your average

10 minutes of boredom because you're feeling lazy or tired. No, this is a persistent feeling of pure vacancy within that leaves you hungry for any sense of meaning, any sense of direction through the seemingly worthless interiors of our minds. We want to do something, anything for it to go away. Unfortunately, this often includes impulsive, reckless and self-destructive behaviors."[26]

"One of the many symptoms of BPD is chronic feelings of emptiness. This isn't your average 10 minutes of boredom because you're feeling lazy or tired. No, this is a persistent feeling of pure vacancy within that leaves you hungry for any sense of meaning, any sense of direction through the seemingly worthless interiors of our minds."[26]

—*Bisma Suleman, a person who suffers from BPD*

Dealing with the fallout of BPD—its causes and its effects—is far-reaching and affects all aspects of daily life. But there is hope. Over the past fifty years, a number of groundbreaking treatments and therapy programs have emerged that have made living with borderline personality disorder a surmountable obstacle instead of a permanent burden.

CHAPTER FOUR

What Is the Treatment for BPD?

When Rebecca was thirteen years old, she tried to take her own life. She had grown up in a violent household and couldn't handle the stress anymore. The local child services authority was called, and she was committed to a psychiatric ward for a brief stay. After a series of tests and appointments with various doctors who worked in inpatient care, she was diagnosed with borderline personality disorder.

Over the next thirteen years, she bounced around from therapist to therapist trying to figure out how to treat her disorder. But because none of the therapists knew enough about BPD, the counseling sessions didn't work. She went on medication, but some of the drugs she took made her symptoms worse. "Like, if [the drugs] treated my impulsivity and anger, [they increased] my suicidal thoughts. If they treated my suicidal thoughts, I [experienced] intensified mood swings.

Therapy can be very helpful for learning how to cope with BPD. It is important for someone to find a therapist who is best suited for their needs.

Medication is really something you have to be patient with," Rebecca later explained.[27]

Finally, when she was twenty-six, she scheduled an appointment with a therapist who focused on treating patients with BPD. It was a perfect fit. "Finding a therapist that specialized in [borderline] personality disorder has been my saving grace," she wrote. "I'm lucky to have found one locally, even though it took me a year and a half after moving here, to find her."[28]

Since discovering her BPD-certified therapist, Rebecca's life improved considerably. She still suffered from mood swings and had panic attacks when she neglected her self-care routine. But she learned to be more mindful about what types of events might trigger a BPD incident and how to prevent emotional outbursts from occurring. She read books about her condition, such as *Mindfulness for Borderline Personality Disorder* by Blaise Aguirre. She even started to be more open about her BPD diagnosis with loved ones to help them understand why she can't always control her reactions and behavior. "People that were close to me were generally accepting and not surprised. It was like giving them an answer to a question they were too respectful to ask," she wrote. "Honestly, saying the diagnosis out loud felt more like I was learning to accept myself for who I am, rather than seeking acceptance from others. I feel like I can finally breathe."[29]

Most of all, Rebecca's outlook on life got better because she learned how to be more confident about her worth as a person. "We're not lost causes. There are a LOT of people and resources who will tell you to run away, we're not worth it, we'll just burn your life down," she wrote. "Loving us is difficult (trust me, it was very hard for even me to love myself) but there are success stories."[30]

Dealing with BPD can feel like an overwhelming burden. But as with many mental disorders, there are healthy, progressive paths to treatment. The most important step is to seek professional help in order to find out what options are available. Most personality disorders are diagnosed after an in-depth interview with a mental health provider or doctor. During the interview, a variety of criteria are used, such as a complete medical exam and a detailed overview of past medical records to see whether BPD runs in the family. Sometimes more fine-tuned questionnaires geared toward BPD patients are administered to determine how serious the condition might be and to rule out other conditions. After a diagnosis is made, a treatment protocol is suggested, ranging from regular talk therapy to inpatient care.

"We're not lost causes. There are a LOT of people and resources who will tell you to run away, we're not worth it, we'll just burn your life down. Loving us is difficult (trust me, it was very hard for even me to love myself) but there are success stories."[30]

—Rebecca, a person who suffers from BPD

PSYCHOTHERAPY

Psychotherapy, also called talk therapy, is an essential treatment approach for BPD. It helps patients focus on their ability to complete daily tasks, manage emotions that might seem out of

The first step of DBT is for the patient to accept their emotions and identity. From there, they are able to learn ways to handle their responses.

whack or uncomfortable, reduce impulsivity, be more aware of feelings and why they occur, and improve relationships. There are five major types of psychotherapy to try. What is suitable for one person might not be suitable for another.

The most widely used and effective treatment option for BPD is called dialectical behavior therapy (DBT), which balances a BPD patient's need for acceptance with the need for change. It uses a skills-based approach to teach people with BPD how to keep their emotions from getting out of hand, manage their moods through mindfulness, tolerate distress or upsetting events, reduce self-destructive behavior, and improve social interactions. DBT includes one-on-one therapy sessions, group skills training sessions, and phone coaching with a therapist as needed. The therapy has been proven to help reduce

Meditate to Soothe

Sitting quietly in a room and contemplating one's presence in the moment might not seem like it'd be an effective solution for a serious psychiatric illness. But in fact, mindful meditation is increasingly being used to treat certain mental health conditions. Intense mood swings are one of the symptoms of BPD. People with BPD can also become fixated on their feelings and, in turn, make negative judgments about both the emotions and themselves. "Unfortunately, this can end up making the emotion feel even more intense. Judgmental thoughts can add other emotions to the mix; if you tell yourself you are weak for feeling sad you may end up feeling both sad and ashamed," says Dr. Kristalyn Salters-Pedneault.

Mindful meditation teaches people to become more aware of what they are feeling before reacting. With that distanced perspective, they can then make informed, healthy decisions about what kind of action to take. For example, in an argument a person with BPD might scream, cry, and throw things immediately. But mindfulness allows them to take a step back, consider what they hope to accomplish in the situation, and maybe wait until a better time to continue the discussion when emotions are less heated.

Kristalyn Salters-Pedneault, "How Mindfulness Meditation Can Help Borderline Personality Disorder," Verywell Mind, September 19, 2019. www.verywellmind.com.

psychiatric hospitalization, substance abuse, explosive anger, interpersonal difficulties, suicidal behavior, and the temptation to drop out of treatment.

"It's essentially a skills-based approach which says that if our patients could do better, they would, but they're lacking skills," explains Dr. Alec Miller, the author of *Dialectical Behavioral Therapy with Suicidal Adolescents*. "It's so easy for us to tell people to stop problematic behaviors but it's better to teach them new skills."[31]

> "It's so easy for us to tell people to stop problematic behaviors but it's better to teach them new skills."[31]
>
> —Dr. Alec Miller, the author of Dialectical Behavioral Therapy with Suicidal Adolescents

Mentalization-based therapy (MBT) is another type of individual or group talk therapy that teaches people with BPD how to make sense of their actions, behaviors, and feelings as well as those of others by prompting them to visualize their interpersonal relationships step-by-step. For example, after a fight breaks out at school, BPD sufferers are taught in therapy to first identify the way they thought and felt during the event. Then they are instructed to create an alternative perspective on the situation. This two-part process helps them learn that their way of thinking isn't the only path forward. It also teaches them to empathize with others' feelings and reactions. As with most therapies, MBT practitioners hope that once patients use mentalization enough times in session, they can put it into practice in real life.

Schema-focused therapy (SFT) focuses on helping BPD sufferers pinpoint and change their deeply ingrained, self-defeating patterns of thoughts, behavior, and emotions, known as schemas.[32] This treatment method proposes that many of the symptoms of BPD are caused by difficult childhood experiences, such as living with an abusive parent, which can lead to poor coping skills later on. In individual or group sessions, the goal of SFT is to help people with BPD break these patterns and form new, healthier ways of existing in the world. For example, an SFT-certified therapist might ask her patient to act out a situation that would normally incite anger. But instead of acting rashly, the patient would try to resolve the situation in a calm, rational manner. In short, SFT implores people to break down their unhelpful ways of thinking in order to form new, positive patterns.

Transference-focused therapy (TFP), also called psychodynamic psychotherapy, is designed to help BPD sufferers understand their emotions and interpersonal problems through the relationship they form with their therapist. Patients can then apply the insights they pick up in counseling to other

STEPPS therapy includes the person diagnosed with BPD as well as his or her family and friends. This form of therapy creates a support group that is able to help a person with BPD in a crisis.

environments, such as a job or school. Sessions are usually held twice a week, and there is no group therapy option.

Finally, systems training for emotional predictability and problem-solving (STEPPS) is a twenty-week course of treatment that involves working in groups. Family members, caregivers, friends, and romantic partners are all encouraged to get involved. There are three phases of treatment. "In the first part, individuals learn that BPD is an 'emotional intensity disorder.' They learn that they aren't fatally flawed, and can learn skills to manage and reduce their symptoms. They also learn the cognitive 'filters' or beliefs that drive their behavior," says Margarita Tartakovsky of Psych Central.[33] In the second phase, BPD sufferers are taught adaptive skills to help them manage the cognitive and emotional effects of their condition. The third phase focuses

Family Connections

Designed by BPD experts Dr. Alan E. Fruzzetti and Dr. Perry D. Hoffman, Family Connections is a twelve-week, NIMH research–backed program for family members of individuals with BPD. Sessions are offered in many languages, hosted in a community setting, and led by NEABPD-trained experts. Participants learn new skills based on DBT teachings, including how to practice mindfulness, engage in open and honest communication, and interact with their loved ones in a healthy manner so that everyone feels validated and feels their needs are being met. For family members who don't live near the treatment center, NEABPD also offers TeleConnections, an over-the-phone version of the program conducted during weekly conference calls.

"First and foremost, what I am struck with is the group members' sincere desire to better understand their loved one's illness and to find tools to cope," participant Anna Warde told *Recovery Today*. "The group is not even halfway through and already there is a powerful feeling of connection and camaraderie. I find myself thinking about the participants throughout the week and I look forward to seeing them and listening to them. Inside, I root for them to know that they can move beyond just surviving."

Anna Warde with Shannon Huggins, LCSW,
"Borderline Personality Disorder:
A View from the Inside,"
Recovery Today, January 2008.
www.borderlinepersonalitydisorder.org.

on setting goals and teaching people with BPD to choose healthy coping mechanisms, such as exercise and meditation, over self-harm behaviors. Throughout STEPPS and any of the other BPD-focused therapies, loved ones are encouraged to take a hands-on approach in contributing to the healing and recovery process.

MEDICATION AND HOSPITALIZATION

Psychotherapies such as DBT have been proven to be a highly effective way of treating BPD. According to the NEABPD, 75 percent of people with BPD treated with DBT improved after a year, and 95 percent of patients improved after two years. But for those people for whom DBT and other therapies haven't been that successful, there are other options.

By 2020, there wasn't an FDA-approved medication that specifically addresses BPD. But people with the condition are often prescribed medicine that targets co-occurring disorders, such as depression, anxiety, and eating disorders. As long as they are part of a doctor- or therapist-sanctioned treatment plan, antidepressants such as Prozac and Effexor can help reduce fluctuations in mood.

For cases that are more advanced or when patients with BPD are a danger to themselves or others, the *American Psychiatric Association Practice Guideline for the Treatment of*

BPD is most commonly treated using a variety of therapies. Antidepressants and mood stabilizers can be prescribed if the patient is diagnosed with other mental illnesses alongside BPD.

Patients with Borderline Personality Disorder suggests inpatient care may be required. There are two types of hospitalization stays: voluntary and involuntary. A voluntary hospitalization occurs when the patient willingly recognizes that he or she is in need of greater care than what is provided through regular therapy sessions. An involuntary stay happens when the patient is unwilling to consider hospital care, but the therapist or other medical professionals have decided a more serious approach is necessary. In cases like this, such as if the patient is suicidal, he or she is committed against his or her will.

At the hospital, patients must attend individual therapy, group sessions, or both. Medication is sometimes administered. Patients are discharged to a day hospital or outpatient treatment to help them transition back into their daily routine once their condition is stable. Programs can last anywhere from a few days to a few months.

COPING AND SUPPORT

Aside from regularly going to scheduled therapy sessions and being consistent with prescribed medication, there are plenty of ways a person with BPD can practice self-care to complement a treatment regimen. Steering clear of drugs and alcohol, getting enough sleep, and maintaining a healthy diet keep the body and mind energized and prepared for whatever might unfold during the day. Exercise, such as running, yoga, or weight training, has been proven to improve mood, decrease anxiety, and reduce stress.

Being aware of emotions and why they occur is also an important skill to cultivate on a daily basis. "Often, you're very emotional today because of something that happened yesterday, because you didn't sleep, because you didn't eat, because of some stress from yesterday," says DBT founder Dr. Marsha Linehan. "[Ask yourself] what are the factors that make you vulnerable to being emotional and how can you change those factors? What is the prompting event, meaning what happened right before? Is that something that you can change?"[34]

> "Often, you're very emotional today because of something that happened yesterday, because you didn't sleep, because you didn't eat, because of some stress from yesterday. What are the factors that make you vulnerable to being emotional and how can you change those factors? What is the prompting event, meaning what happened right before? Is that something that you can change?"[34]
>
> —DBT founder Dr. Marsha Linehan

Participating in positive, calming, confidence-boosting hobbies such as painting, drawing, dancing, knitting, or even listening to soothing music can help regulate moods and invite peace into the daily routine. Journaling has been shown to help people with a personality disorder process their thoughts, prevent emotional buildup, and keep track of their recovery progress. There are also self-guided workbooks available that offer exercises specifically for people working through BPD. These include *The Borderline Personality Disorder Workbook:*

Mindful activities can help someone with BPD better understand her thoughts and emotions. Activities such as knitting and painting can be effective coping strategies.

An Integrative Program to Understand and Manage Your BPD by Daniel J. Fox, PhD, and *The Dialectical Behavior Therapy Skills Workbook: Practical DBT Exercises for Learning Mindfulness,*

Interpersonal Effectiveness, Emotion Regulation and Distress Tolerance by Matthew McKay, PhD, Jeffrey C. Wood, PsyD, and Jeffrey Brantley, MD.

Perhaps most importantly—for BPD patients and their loved ones—finding a steady support group is essential to a less bumpy road on the way to recovery. Enduring the ups and downs of BPD can be confusing, maddening, and even life-threatening at times. But with the right treatment regimen and plenty of encouragement, healing is possible.

Source Notes

Introduction: Finding a Path to Healing

1. Molly Burford, "The Power of the Proper Diagnosis," *Glamour*, August 6, 2019. www.glamour.com.

2. Burford, "The Power of the Proper Diagnosis."

3. Burford, "The Power of the Proper Diagnosis."

4. Burford, "The Power of the Proper Diagnosis."

Chapter 1: What Is BPD?

5. Quoted in Melissa Valliant, "Most Accurate Article on BPD We Have Read—Kudos!" *NEABPD*, 2020. www.borderlinepersonalitydisorder.org.

6. Quoted in Jessica Migala, "Does Borderline Personality Disorder Affect Women More Than Men?" *Everyday Health*, April 12, 2018. www.everydayhealth.com.

7. Quoted in Migala, "Does Borderline Personality Disorder Affect Women More than Men?"

8. Quoted in "Teen Moodiness, or Borderline Personality Disorder?" *New York Times*, February 25, 2010. https://consults.blogs.nytimes.com.

9. Quoted in "Teen Moodiness, or Borderline Personality Disorder?"

10. Quoted in Caroline Miller, "What Is Borderline Personality Disorder?" *Child Mind Institute*, 2020. www.childmind.org.

11. Quoted in Miller, "What Is Borderline Personality Disorder?"

Chapter 2: What Are the Symptoms and Causes of BPD?

12. Quoted in "Teen Moodiness, or Borderline Personality Disorder?"

13. John M. Grohol, "Borderline Personality Disorder Symptoms," *Psych Central*, January 14, 2020. www.psychcentral.com.

14. Quoted in Miller, "What Is Borderline Personality Disorder?"

15. Kristalyn Salters-Pedneault, "The Link Between Borderline Personality Disorder and Anger," *Verywell Mind*, August 16, 2019. www.verywellmind.com.

16. Grohol, "Borderline Personality Disorder Symptoms."

17. Kristalyn Salters-Pedneault, "Suicidality in Borderline Personality Disorder," *Verywell Mind*, November 10, 2019. www.verywellmind.com.

Chapter 3: How Does BPD Affect Daily Life?

18. Erika Lee, "What I Want You to Know About Borderline Personality Disorder," *HuffPost*, November 1, 2019. www.huffpost.com.

19. Lee, "What I Want You to Know About Borderline Personality Disorder."

20. Lee, "What I Want You to Know About Borderline Personality Disorder."

21. Quoted in "I Loved, Lived With, and Lost My Mother to Borderline Personality Disorder," *Salon*, February 29, 2016. www.salon.com.

22. Quoted in Jane E. Brody, "An Emotional Hair Trigger, Often Misread," *New York Times*, June 15, 2009. www.nytimes.com.

23. Erin Johnston, "Borderline Personality Disorder (BPD) and Employment," *Verywell Mind*, March 4, 2020. www.verywellmind.com.

24. Kristalyn Salters-Pedneault, "Legal Issues and Borderline Personality Disorder," *Verywell Mind*, September 25, 2019. www.verywellmind.com.

25. Salters-Pedneault, "Legal Issues and Borderline Personality Disorder."

Source Notes Continued

26. Bisma Suleman, "10 Things People with Borderline Personality Disorder Want You to Know," *National Alliance on Mental Illness*, August 5, 2019. www.nami.org.

Chapter 4: What Is the Treatment for BPD?

27. "True Story: I Have Borderline Personality Disorder," *Yes and Yes*, October 2, 2017. www.yesandyes.org.

28. "True Story: I Have Borderline Personality Disorder."

29. "True Story: I Have Borderline Personality Disorder."

30. "True Story: I Have Borderline Personality Disorder."

31. Quoted in Miller, "What Is Borderline Personality Disorder?"

32. "Borderline Personality Disorder," *Mayo Clinic*, July 17, 2019. www.mayoclinic.org.

33. Margarita Tartakovsky, "Borderline Personality Disorder Treatment," *Psych Central*, October 22, 2019. www.psychcentral.com.

34. Quoted in "Marsha Linehan - Strategies for Emotion Regulation," *YouTube*, April 14, 2017. www.youtube.com.

For Further Research

Books

Cherese Cartlidge, *Teens and Suicide*. San Diego, CA: ReferencePoint Press, 2017.

Daniel J. Fox, PhD, *The Borderline Personality Disorder Workbook: An Integrative Program to Understand and Manage Your BPD*. Oakland, CA: New Harbinger, 2019.

Tammy Gagne, *Dealing with Self-Injury Disorder*. San Diego, CA: ReferencePoint Press, 2020.

John G. Gunderson and Perry D. Hoffman, *Beyond Borderline: True Stories of Recovery from Borderline Personality Disorder*. Oakland, CA: New Harbinger, 2016.

Internet Sources

Blaise Aguirre, MD, "What Teens Want to Know About Borderline Personality Disorder," *McLean Hospital*, September 8, 2019. www.mcleanhospital.org.

Benedict Carey, "Expert on Mental Illness Reveals Her Own Fight," *New York Times*, June 23, 2011. www.nytimes.com.

Caroline Miller, "What Is Borderline Personality Disorder?" *Child Mind*, n.d. https://childmind.org.

Polaris Teen Center, "Borderline Personality Disorder in Teens: What You Need to Know," *Polaris Teen*, June 14, 2018. https://polaristeen.com.

Websites

National Education Alliance for Borderline Personality Disorder (NEABPD)
www.borderlinepersonalitydisorder.com

The NEABPD website is a resource for families and people in recovery that includes the latest facts, stories from people suffering from BPD, treatment resources, and other links to informative BPD-related sites.

National Institute of Mental Health (NIMH)
www.nimh.nih.gov/health/topics
/borderline-personality-disorder/index.shtml

The NIMH website has an online portal for people suffering from BPD and their loved ones that contains the latest statistics, brochures, and fact sheets about the condition, information about clinical trials, and other educational resources.

Treatment and Research Advancements for Borderline Personality Disorder (TARA)
www.tara4bpd.org

The TARA website is a place for people with BPD and their loved ones that includes the latest facts, information about treatment options, and links to stories about BPD in the media.

Index

Index Continued

Image Credits

About the Author

Alexis Burling has written dozens of articles and books for young readers on a variety of topics, including current events and famous people, nutrition and fitness, careers and money management, relationships, and cooking. She is also a book critic with reviews of both adult and young adult books, author interviews, and other industry-related articles published in the *New York Times*, *Washington Post*, *San Francisco Chronicle*, *Chicago Tribune*, and more. Burling lives in Portland, Oregon, with her husband.